Summer Activity Book

Compiled and illustrated by Leila Bassir

First published 2020 by Laughing Linnet Publications

This Book Belongs To Nature Explorer

In this book, you will find:

- Information about how to do a nature walk, things to take and things to remember
- A summary of the 6 nature directions
- Nature activity pages with spotter lists and check sheets
- Drawing, scrapbook and nature note pages

Remember to have fun, and
Happy Nature Walking!

Do not wait for the storms to pass

...

Learn to dance in the rain!

L Bassir
CEO

www.mynaturenook.com

Facebook: TheNatureNook/
Instagram: my.nature.nook

My Nature Nook
Explore. Discover. Play

Those who love Nature,

will find beauty

everywhere!

Aristotle

What's Inside?

Remember

- Always make sure when you explore, that an adult knows where you are
- Always take care near rocks, cliffs and water
- Always take any litter home
- Always be respectful of Nature

Summer...

Summer arrives every year, bringing colourful flowers, buzzy bees, beautiful butterflies, sparkly leaves; singing birds, teeming ponds, and happy, sunny days... There is so much and everyone loves something different.

What makes it special to you?

Some ideas to think about, are:

- Colours
- Smells
- Sounds
- Sights
- Textures
- Tastes
- Weather
- Games
- Food
- Clothing

Get Ready...

Summer may be beautiful with its bright colours, cheerful sounds leaves and blue skies, but it still helps to be prepared and to dress sensibly and take fluids or snacks when you go outside. So, have a little think about what you might need.

What will YOU need for your Summer Nature Walk?

Some things you might need are:

- Light clothes
- Light coat
- Walking boots
- Sunhat
- Suncream
- Insect repellent
- Waterproofs
- Water
- Snacks

Get Set...

Okay! We're ready and know all our favourite Summer things... We know what we need to take with us on our Quest... Now we need to decide where to do it!

So, where will you have your Adventure?

A few places you might go, are:

- Garden
- Park
- Forest
- Hedgerow
- Meadow
- Riverside
- Lakeside
- Moorland
- Allotment
- Canal side

Go...!

Fern Mary Martenez (handwritten)

Summer is a treasure trove for the worthy, brave Explorer. All you must do is keep your eyes open, your ears sharp and your mind alert to spot the treasures you are seeking.

What do YOU expect to find on your Summer Nature Walk?

Some things you might find are:

- Leaves
- Flowers
- Fruit
- Lichens
- Moss
- Butterflies
- Birds
- Animals
- Babies
- Bugs

fern   fern (handwritten)

The Six Directions

When you are new to doing a Nature Walk, it can be very confusing working out where you need to look and what you need to do. There is so much stuff happening around you - where do you start?!

To help you out, I have devised 6 Nature Walk Directions:

These directions are:

- Above - up in the sky
- Canopy - the tops of the trees, mountaintop, clifftop
- Surroundings - side-to-side, tree trunks, mountainside
- Shrubbery - tall plants, bushes, tall grasses
- Undergrowth - small plants, ferns, soil, rocks
- Below - underneath your feet

Remember to look and listen for all the things on the previous page:

Leaves, flowers, grasses, ferns, butterflies, bees, other bugs, birds, animals, lichens, moss, stones.

Are you ready?

It is Time for Your Quest!

Lets enjoy some Nature Activities...

Summer brings with it beautiful, colourful flowers. Can you spot these flowers in a country hedgerow?

Dog roses
Found some!

Honeysuckle
Found some!

Elderflowers
Found some!

Here are some flowers you might find in a park. Can you match them to their names.

Linden   Horse chestnut   Rhododendron

What other flowers can you find and name?

Can you spot these flowers in a woodland?

Agrimony
Found some!

Foxglove
Found some!

Betony
Found some!

Here are a few meadow flowers you might find. Can you match them to their names.

Stitchwort   Yarrow   Clover

What other flowers can you find? Draw them here.

As well as flowers, the trees are full of green leaves. How many can you find?

Beech
Found some!

Birch
Found some!

Sycamore
Found some!

Here are a few more leaves. Can you match them to their names.

Willow   Alder   Hawthorn

Can you find a nice leaf to do a leaf rubbing?

They say the arrival of these birds signals the arrival of summer.
Can you hear them and see them?

Swift
Spotted!

Swallow
Spotted!

Martin
Spotted!

Spend an hour bird-watching in a park, garden, or during a nature walk.

What other birds can you see? What are they doing?

It is fun spotting ducks and on a river or lakeside nature walk. Can you spot these ones?

Mallard
Found one!

Tufted duck
Found one!

Pochard
Found one!

How well do you know your other water birds? Can you correctly identify these?

Moorhen   Coot   Cormorant

What other water birds can you find? Draw them here.

Summer brings with it a flurry of insect activity. Can you spot these?

Dragonfly
Spotted one!

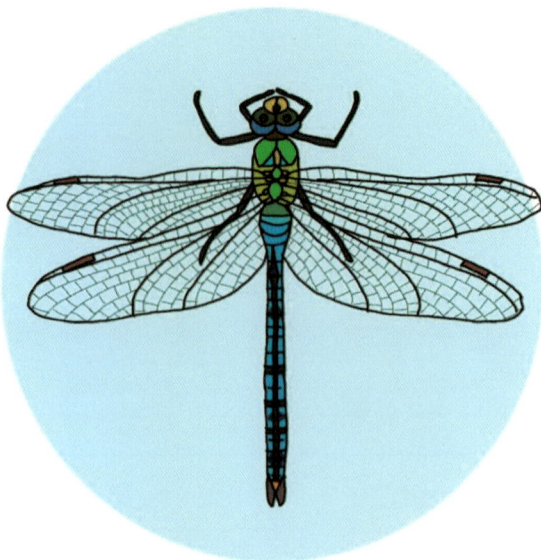

Damselfly
Spotted one!

Mayfly
Spotted one!

Here are some insects you might hear. Can you match them to their names.

Grasshopper   Cricket   Katyid

Do you know how these insects make their sounds? See if you can find out and write your answer here.

- -

- -

- -

- -

Summer is a great time for spotting butterflies, too. Can you spot these three common butterflies?

Comma
Spotted one!

Peacock
Spotted one!

Red Admiral
Spotted one!

Underneath the soil, even the ants are busy with their babies.
Do you know which ant is which?

  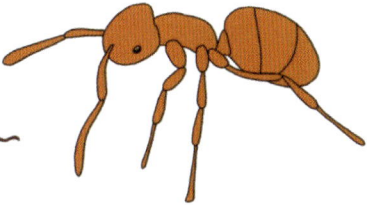

Wood ant   Meadow ant   Garden ant

What other insects can you find?

- -

- -

- -

- -

- -

What are your favourite summertime trees and flowers? Draw some of them here.

Now lets draw some wildlife! Draw your favourite summertime birds, bugs or animals here.

Summer is a very noisy season, as everyone is singing. How many birds or insects can you hear? Can you describe the sounds you hear?

E.g. bird song can be melodic, chirpy, whistling, wheezy

Summer also brings with it many beautiful colours. How many summer colours can you think of, see and name? How can you describe them?

For example: green – bright, fresh, pale, fizzy, sparkly

Answers!

Answers given from right to left

Park flowers - rhododendron, linden, horse chestnut

Meadow flowers - yarrow, stitchwort, clover

Leaves - hawthorn, willow, alder

Insects - katydid, grasshopper, cricket

Ants - garden ant, wood ant, meadow ant

Water birds - cormorant, coot, moorhen

Thank You!

I hope you enjoyed your Quest and I am so excited you to chose my book to take along on your adventure!

Did you have fun?

Did you see more than you imagined you would see?

Are you glad you went outdoors?

Yay! Well done you!

Now I have one last task...

- If you enjoyed this activity book, it would be absolutely fantastic if you could leave a review and tell your fellow explorers so they can use it too!
- And... don't forget to share stories and pictures of your adventures #mynaturenook on instagram; and visit My Nature Nook (www.mynaturenook.com)for more quests and adventures!

CERTIFICATE OF ACHIEVEMENT

THIS IS PRESENTED TO

- -

MY NATURE NOOK
Nature Club

For completing a summer nature walk and
successfully meeting all the requirements
for the Summer Explorer's Nature Badge.

LEILA BASSIR
CEO & Founder

- - - - - - - - - - - - / - - - - - / - - - - - - - -

Printed in Great Britain
by Amazon